HUMAN TiME

인간의 시간

Human Time

by Kim Haengsook

Translated by Léo-Thomas Brylowski, Hannah Hertzog, Susan K, Jiyoon Lee, Joanne Park, Soeun Seo, Soohyun Yang

Black Ocean
Boston · Chicago

Black Ocean
P.O. Box 52030
Boston, MA 02205
blackocean.org

Cover Art and Design by Abby Haddican | abbyhaddican.com
Book Design by Taylor D. Waring | taylordwaring.com

ISBN: 978-1-93-956869-4
Library of Congress Control Number: 2022945724

This book is published with the support of the Literature Translation Institute of Korea (LTI Korea).

FIRST EDITION

Printed in Canada.

CONTENTS

3

4

TRANSLATORS' NOTE:

Usually, an individual translator or a group of cotranslators embark on a project on a single title, working on it independently for several years. The translator may remark on how a text called out to them to be translated, describing the relationship through the language of intimacy. The longer and deeper the translator dives into a text, the more they become attached to it. Sometimes the translator forms a bond and association with the author so strong that the translator may be taken to be the author's double. Or an imposter. A translator might have a sense of ownership for an author's representation to the extent that they might feel it necessary not only to embody the text but also to become possessed by the author. Anyone who has taken this plunge knows that the exorcism from this state can be very painful, possibly resulting in leaving the translator disembodied.

For some years I taught a stylistics class comparing recently published translations of Korean fiction and poetry in English to the source texts. Patterns emerge that differentiate the two major genres: poetry and fiction. Like measuring the transparency of vellum versus plastic wrap, the voice, style, and strategies employed by prose translators tends to be more opaque than that of the translators of poetry. Another reason translation strategies might be easier to identify in prose rather than in poetry is that most prose translations, at least from Korean to English, are done by a single translator. Except for the partnership of Bruce and Ju-Chan Fulton, I cannot think of any recent Korean to English fiction translations credited to more than a single translator. In poetry translation, conversely, it is just as likely that a book has been translated by multiple translators, often working as a team. The poet Kim Hyesoon's (Kim Hyesun 김혜순) *Han chan ŭi pulgŭn kŏul* 한 잔의 붉은 거울, translated into English as *A Drink of Red Mirror*, is an exceptional case of co-translation[1]. Translated by a class at Arizona State University, but credited primarily to Shin Jiwon, Lauren Albin, and Sue Hyon Bae, this book challenges not only ideas of the practice of translation, but also the idea of ownership and production of translated texts. Individual poems are credited to different translators but according to an interview by the translators and the introduction to the book, this was very much a class project, a whole-team effort, which was as complicated and frustrating as it was rewarding[2].

Many questions emerged about a process of translation that included so many collaborators. What happens when that sense of embodiment or intimacy in translation practice is shared communally? Does that association and bond between author and translator dissipate? What happens when you parcel out a book in sections and then work on its translation as a large team, editing and shaping the voice and style of the translated text together? Just as one can interpret something otherwise, translators too can translate otherwise, but what happens when we interpret together, translate together? What

---

1   Kim Hyesoon and Jiwon Shin and Lauren Albin and Sue Hyon Bae, *A Drink of Red Mirror*, (Notre Dame: Action Books, 2019). 김혜순 <한 잔의 붉은 거울> (서울: 민음사, 2004).

2   Lauren Albin, Matt Reeck, and Sue Hyon Bae, "How Should We Review Translations? Part II," *Asymptote*, September, 25 2019, https://www.asymptotejournal.com/blog/2019/09/25/how-should-we-review-translations-part-ii/#more-21479

new riches are there to be discovered? Could communal translation as a practice help liberate the language of the text from the world of property relations? Could it unlock other forms of cooperation for use in other modes of artistic production? Because translation confounds and complicates concepts like originality, authenticity, authorship, and ownership, it is an artistic mode riddled with anxiety—anxiety not only for translators who must wrestle with these concepts but also for a world that defines art in terms of ownership and commodity relations.

The fact that *A Drink of Red Mirror* was translated by so many people made it largely ineligible for awards and prizes: too many spoons in the soup. No one knows who added the salt and lime: no hierarchy and no master chef to worship. In a project completed over several years and in multiple versions, it is hard to track who is responsible for what. Instead of becoming possessed and then left disembodied, the translator cannot become a possession and can possess nothing. Whenever translators say *my* author or *my* book, what they are really saying is *myself*. Instead of an I-me or an I-we relationship, a translator working on a joint project is in a I-we-thou relationship. This is a great mode for translation, as a priori, translations exist through collaboration and in multiples. Just as there is no one, single inventor of language, books do not owe their existence to any particular individuals, their backgrounds, or their experiences. The cults of personality and hero-worship translators build around other translators is a symptom of the inequities of the system. Death of the author might require the death of the translator as well. But translation by community doesn't require anyone to die, since no one person is responsible. This does not mean they are made to be invisible. Instead, it shows that they are willing to work in unison, leaving their ego at the door in order to breathe new life into the text.

The poems in this book are a selected volume by the contemporary poet Kim Haengsook (Kim Haengsuk 김행숙). They were chosen by the author herself from her books, which span a twenty-year career. The majority of the poems were communally translated and workshopped. Although each poem is attributed to the translator or translators who were responsible for the initial translation, all the revisions and subsequent craft choices were made collaboratively as a team, often by vote.

The work of Kim Haengsook is a perfect match for this type of project. Poetry that requires a strong sense of voice, particularly poems that incorporate a persona or personas like the work of Kim Yideum, Kim Min Jeong, or Park Jun, requires the translator or translators to create a character or characters. This means that the diction and syntactic choices must remain consistent with the strength of the author's voice. Kim Haengsook's speakers are ethereal and disembodied. Her work is imagistic, philosophical, and meditative. These poems expand in space rather than progress through time. Poems that rely heavily on imagery and rhetoric give the translator much more flexibility, but Kim Haengsook's poems deal in what she calls "precise ambiguity (정확한 애매함)."[3] Precise ambiguity functions not through direct contrast, but rather by giving language to the in-between. The difficulty then is in having to capture this paradox, the precisely ambiguous. In an interview

---

3   Kim Haengsook, "[A Conversation with Kim Haengsook] "Precise Ambiguity" and the Power of the In-Between, by Jake Levine, *Korean Literature Now*, (Seoul: Vol. 39, Spring 2018).

I conducted with her over email for *Korea Literature Now*[4] in 2018, Kim wrote,

> To my mind, the body in a poetic state is less like a factory which produces something, and more like a corrugated steel roof on which raindrops fall. A steel roof does not make sounds on its own accord, but raindrops, also, don't make a sound unless they meet with something like a steel roof. It's impossible to know what might come to pass when the outside world is approached and accessed in such a way. This is why it's possible to say something like, "We do not write new things in poetry, but rather become new by writing poetry."

Like raindrops banging on a roof, having many interlocutors involved in interpreting and directing the English language together, in chorus, made it possible to find a linguistic fit for her work. Even though you know it is made from the crash of individual drops, translating together, in harmony, is like the sound of falling rain. It is neither here nor there; it saturates, permeates everything.

We'd like to thank Kim Haengsook for putting together this collection and for giving us the opportunity to translate her work. We'd also like to thank the Literature Translation Institute of Korea for their support and *Water Stone Review*, *Tinderbox*, *Korean Literature Now*, *Puerto Del Sol*, Action Books Blog, *Acta Koreana*, and *Lana Turner* for first publishing work from this collection.

—Jake Levine, Moon Country Series Editor

---

4   Kim Haengsook, "[A Conversation" ibid.

I

HUMAN TIME

Tread on us and fall in love
like waves.

We're deep
and break easily.

Time, we're always in the thick of it.

APRIL 16, 1914

It's the date of my birth.
I'm a person who still hasn't died, so
I'm a person with many dead friends.
My dead friends didn't leave me in the 21st century.
It's more like I was the one who left my dead friends
to come here from far away.
Like I was swept to the end of the world
today is April 16, 2014.

HOWEVER

However, when I turn away

can I keep walking away from you?

When I step back into the world where I can't see your back, a world
filled only with things I never loved appears before me.

The world where you don't exist.

However, a world where I'm not that different from the dead, a world
where everyone shares the memories of the dead, a world where
everyone is not that different from the dead.

However, I got on the bus fine, went to the store easily, and found the
toilet without difficulty.

Those weren't the hard things.

You walk toward me with the sun on your back like a huge cyst, and if
the person walking toward me is really you, then I walk straight ahead.

Like a huge, busting sac of pus
this world is so beautiful it frightens me.

LITTLE HOUSE

Let's have a reset. God finally made a decision.

Obeying His words, white snow fell, white snow fell, white snow fell
night and day . . . erasing every footprint in the world. How beautiful.
But . . . this so-called God's vision grew large and distant from looking at
the vast world. The little house became like an eyelash he couldn't see.
Long long ago an old woman lived alone in a tiny house that looked like
a lost pretty shoe. Time passed. Before she knew it, she began to move
slow, her eyesight worsened, and her memory began to fail. Her life was
like a handful of barley. In one world an old woman made the fire every
day, and in another world, an old woman extinguished the fire's last
embers. If God were to compare these two moments, would they split
like a fork in the road—one toward the forest and the other toward the
sea? Do the sky and earth begin to grow closer again when they are the
furthest apart? Do they reunite? When God fondly looks down, does
the world become one beautiful and seamless painting? As though **what
has been forgotten is suddenly remembered, snow begins to fall. But
this time it's black and falls aslant.**

THE FUTURE 1984

Even with nothing written in it, the book was a compromising possession.

—George Orwell, *1984*

The river Orwell still runs . . .

Arthur Blair's shadow was thrown over and over into the river Orwell. Arthur Blair became the writer George Orwell. But Arthur Blair's shadow didn't follow the current. Staring at his shadow that resisted the current, the writer was seized by a strange feeling. Although it's said in both east and west that life flows like river water, life's dregs pool like puddles.

The first, second, third, and fourth industrial revolution swept through the world . . . swapping out landscapes like broken windows. If you can number the river water, if you can cut it like you cut fabric to sell, negotiate a price per unit, split it into north and south, then each withering person watching dusk fall on the purple river is not really a person. They're a cliff.

George Orwell wrote *1984* in 1948. . . .

And he died in 1950. Each night my friend George Orwell coughed, his phlegm and blood boiled, and his bent shadow stretched into the most distant future 1984. . . . Comrade Orwell, in 1984, 1994, 2004, and 2014, in my 20's, my 30's, and my 40's, I was in Korea. People are like broken records, saying every ten years even the rivers and mountains change, but things not taken by the river's flow, things not swept with the passage of time, they stiffen up and stand in some future fog like canes that belong to stubborn old men. More solid than ghosts, you can touch them. And 1984 is open like a new book someone stopped reading.

So you're on your way home, carrying a book you just bought. In the future . . .

"This book will put you in danger." Orwell whispers, "If a book is a compromising possession, then we will be compromised, and if we are compromised then the book is even more compromising. This suspicion will continue, become continuous, it will deepen, deepening, and your life will uproot. No, you deny it. If the future is not present, how do you accept it? How can you fight the future and say you've won or lost?"

UNDERGROUND TRAVELER 2084

1.   Night light and daylight pour out of the same fountain.

I've almost become the underground. The underground is a worn-out world. As I wander a hundred years watching the new world wear down, my body spores into a mold that aspires into the air. My body becomes humidity and chill . . . becomes like ambiance, a feeling, or a mood; something hard to express in words. People walk around like machines. Directional arrows float in their eyes like bright baby goldfish.

I become rails, a flame, darkness, a train, stairways, a station attendant, lockers, Mozart, Vivaldi. I'm retro. Some things past are bound to return. "I'm looking for a missing child. A six-year-old girl. Wearing a baby blue dress and white tights. 90 years have passed. Her clothes and face must be dirty like the poorest beggar." I've become the clipped shadow of that six-year-old girl. If her shadow remains, she can return. "This is a bad dream!" you scream as you rub the white face you found inside your black hair.

2.   And day darkness and night darkness are homogenous.

We took shelter from storms and blizzards in the subway. We descended into the deepest darkness and imagined life after Earth's destruction. What we imagined became reality. The reality of an underground traveler. Traveling happens between reality and dreams, between life and death. If nine people are alive then one is dead, and if nine people are visible, one can't be seen. That's how it goes. "This must be a bad dream," you mumble as you feel around the black face you found inside your white hair. But sometimes isn't one person alive and nine are dead? Sometimes isn't one person visible and nine can't be seen?

Are you a living person? I'm not so sure. For every one thing I know, there are nine things I don't. That's how it goes. I consider every country's metro to be a place to stay for eternal wanderers, for those who make immortal itineraries. As soon as I think I know who those countless organisms lined up on the underground platforms are, I realize I don't. But then again, I can see through them. After a bomb strapped to the chest of a man exploded, my world collapsed. Each person became everybody's night.

DEAR ANGEL

I heard there's a chair in heaven. I heard there's a left and a right. Sometimes I think what she means is that if something exists in heaven that also exists in this world it must be good

and then sometimes I think that what she means is that if something exists in this world that also exists in heaven it must be bad. Oh moonlight, you're like an echo. The tail blurs . . . light and echo . . . trembles. First I think moonlight is good for wrapping secrets

and then I think moonlight is good for unwrapping secrets. Moonlight is a good light to softly kneel in. Moonlight is a good light to love in. And moonlight is a good light to die in.

Tonight the world is filled with light good enough for the wings of an angel to get soaked with and, really, it feels like there's no outside to this world. I said there are trains drawing curves underground in the city and I said in the train there are long chairs. I told her the story about how the whites of the eyes of the people who sit on long chairs disappear. It's as if they're dead like people in heaven.

Blowing warm breath into her snowflake ears, I whispered stories of people who kill each other even in their dreams.

Do you love humanity? I asked. I've been waiting for the response.

THE HOUSE OF BEING

Like a silence still not silent
like an entrance into silence
that mouth shape is a synonym for someone who waits at the entrance
a heart on the verge of collapse
just a little more, convincing herself to wait just a little more.
She is like the dampness that sticks to the broom she uses
to sweep the floor of a house made of ice
which was once made of water
until thin layers of ice began to grow like moss.
That mouth shape revealed
someone whose words recede like the tide
a silence not yet silent
a narrow entrance into silence.
When that mouth shape appeared at dinner time I dropped my spoon
but she didn't notice
and the spoon was caved in just enough to scoop only a little at a time
and it was bent.
Enlarge the spoon and it becomes a shovel.
Shovels are good for digging the earth.
Between earth, water, fire, and air, a time that nears earth
like when autumn turns an earthy color
and the sunset turns an earthy color
and my face turns an earthy color

that mouth shape, that mouth that hasn't left the mouth
those words that haven't been spoken by the mouth
the corners of silence
the cries of a baby that's not yet cried.

JANUARY 1ST

There's something mysterious about seeing a balloon fly into the sky. The way a rubber balloon no bigger than a palm slowly swells with air, how it slowly grows thinner . . . the way it's lost forever the moment it loses hold of a child's clasped hand. . . .

If we could do that by cupping the palms of our hands on a cold winter night. . . .

Street people will rise and float above roofs, people whose hearts have long been filled with air. Above a roof are a street vendor who lost his cart and a drunk who lost his wallet. The two briefly freeze in the air like phantoms. "I didn't know where to go and my feet wouldn't budge." "I don't know how to get home."

"Hey brother, can you spare a cigarette?" If we could light a fire by rubbing our palms together on a cold winter night. . . .

Each one of us is like a long, pointed flame. If we look at the ashes flying into the air like the tails we hide, today must be January 1st. The same as last year. I solicited someone I'd never seen before on the street. He looked at me with a sad face, like the mirror I looked into that morning.

UNIFICATION OBSERVATORY 2015

We went to see North Korean land.
We went to see something unseen.
In truth, we went to get a breath of cold air.
We went to the Sonata for a change of scenery.
"That's north," someone said.
"Don't we say that when pointing out stars in the night sky?"
Then you snobbishly quoted Lukacs.
"Happy were those ages when the light of the stars illuminated all
possible paths."
When it was my turn to speak
I wanted to give some witty reply
but a . . . ah . . . ahh-CHOO, a sneeze burst out instead.
We tried so hard to make each other laugh that day.

GATEKEEPER

My job is to say, "You can't do that here."
My job is to reject your goals.
My job is to reject you the next day, too.
My job is to wait for you
the day after the next day so I can reject you.
My job is to wait for you
the day after the next day and end up loving you.
So my job is to reject my love.

I write, "I won't cry because of my vocation." Sometimes when I write
in my diary, I cry.

ADAM'S JOKE

What to do about this pain 30, 40, 50 centimeters from my body? If it's a headache, how to bring back the head that's dropped 50, 60, 70 centimeters away from me? 70, 80 centimeters. . . . If the head is running from pain, 80, 90 centimeters. . . . In truth, if the head is going towards pain, if we're all connected to pain, if pain is our central control and the lung capacity of all the citizens and the silence's horizon, then hold the head tight or tie it up in a compression band or pour baptismal water over its crown or plant a pistol to its temple like the sapling of an apple tree or

If all actions taken with the head are emergencies, first I must find the head. 1 meter, 2 meters. . . . If the head starts to escape from sight, it will want to jump the wall, then cross the river, then the ocean. If the aching head decides its own path, it will roll far . . . far . . . far away. If it hasn't thought about what's ahead, it won't think about what gets left behind. If I was made only from things that were left behind, would I forget myself entirely? If there's something to say that I remember but nearly forgot, I need to write it down before I forget again. Could you remember it for me?

If I try to speak, words don't come out easily. People ask me worried questions when I try my best to speak and the words don't come out. "Are you sick? If it's a stomachache, please vomit. If you want to vomit, what do you want to vomit? If you think you're going to vomit, what're the things you think you're going to vomit? What did you smell? What exactly did you see?"

Who the hell is this person who questions and questions and questions? If at first he lowers his head like a social worker to examine my wounds, it's like he's a detective who fished a crime from my wounds by lifting his head. If he's exploiting my weaknesses, first I must know what my weaknesses are. If I want to confess a crime, first I must know what crime to confess. If I say my heart hurts, it's like he'll ask me to show him my heart. If I say I lost my heart, it's like he'll say that he'll find it for me. Even if he speaks kindly, it's like I shouldn't say thank you. If I speak, I think only of words I probably shouldn't say, so I stay silent. If the silence lengthens, that long silence belongs to those who wait. Time flows on, uncaring. Gets paved beneath the sunset. Belongs to those who died. If that kind man starts speaking for me, it's like I've died. Like I'm listening to my own voice from another day.

THIS WORLD

Since I've already put this in this box, I can't put this in the box over there.*

These are your shoes.
Walk, run. There's no reason to peek at the world over there
if the box is big enough.
The policeman in hot pursuit
and the thief being pursued run like hell.
Shake the box and the thief pursues the policeman
but all they did was switch clothes.
At night you fall asleep
clutching your shoes to your chest like they're the Bible.
My baby, sleep well and sweet.
All rivers run to the sea, yet the sea is never full.**
I'm just a shoe factory worker.
I work putting new shoes into new boxes.
Into the box into the box into the box into the box. . . .
Ugh, this is endless.
This is deep, deep darkness.
Put your hand into the darkness and feel around.
These are your shoes.

*Hwang Jeong-eun, "The Smiling Man"
**Ecclesiastes 1:7

"METAMORPHOSIS" (EPILOGUE)

I went to Meran for treatment.
Each night, I took my clothes off and stepped on the scale.
One night
all I had left was 55 kilograms.

After stripping me completely off of the scale
that 0.0 kilogram shadow
slid to the bottom of the stairs and lay down like a 55-kilogram bug.
Dreaming a long dream
to one day wake up squirming in your bed.
My finale, a 55-kilogram shit.
I'll shit and disappear without leaving a spot of shade.

Before then, before then
I'm holding it in
frantically writing everything that must be written.

March 17, 1924*
Franz Kafka

*This was also the day Kafka wrote "Josephine the Singer, or the Mouse Folk." It's impossible to tell which one he wrote first.

METAMORPHOSIS

I like to point to Kafka's "Metamorphosis" as the most
autobiographical novella ever written.
  —Jonathan Franzen

Kafka wrote two versions of the story of a man who woke up one morning as a bug. One version became known throughout the world, but according to the author, this wasn't the complete story of the metamorphosis. The following is a record of the author's grievances.

As if waking up in the middle of the metamorphosis, how much of the bug was Gregor Samsa? What human traces were left in the bug? Why did the father, the mother, and his little sister remember the bug as a shameful part of the family that had to be hidden? Why couldn't the bug completely escape Gregor Samsa's life? Even if the bug had wanted to live a different life in a different place as a different kind of being, was it the failure of Gregor Samsa that after transformation, while locked inside Gregor Samsa's soul, the bug was hurt by the same people that lived in the same house as Gregor Samsa?

Was it a case of the bug's indignity? Or was it that stale and triumphant repertoire of a humanism that claims "even worms will turn." Where did the bugs for bugs' sake go? As a 55 kg human, Gregor Samsa was a shrimp. But anyone who stood in front of 55 kg of bone, flesh, and blood newly formed into a giant bug would shriek, recoil in horror, and fall flat on their ass. In other words, seeing the bug would make anyone look ridiculous. If you just saw an extraterrestrial organism, you would want to spread the news all over the universe, but you would also become paralyzed with fear and excitement. Your whole body would shake, especially your jaw, *clack, clack, clack.*

I'm the dream of the perfect bug.

Humans have long wanted to be fishermen who caught human-size fish, but just imagining a bug the exact size and frame of a human makes people want to piss their pants. When you sleep you dream of whales. When I dream, I dream of bugs.

One morning I woke up as a bug. The bug fit me perfectly. I wasn't lonely anymore. If I stretched out, I guess I would've been about 2 meters long. *Now, let's start to move a bit.* The bug's senses were awakened when the bug began to move. A bug is a bug. The miraculous pleasure that dwells in tautologies is pure. I crawled down from that bed stained with a nasty human stench and began to explore the floor, ceiling, and four walls that made up this simple space as if it was new. I finally arrived on a different planet. Gravitational force applied to me in a different way. The reflection of my silhouette on the window seemed to be made of fog and light and riddles. It was mystifying to watch. Another world opened up to me.

A while later the door to my room, *clink,* opened from the outside. I tried to find with my eyes the change in the round handle. I was more sensitive and nimble. *Mother, I don't see Gregor. Did he leave home? Mother, I want to run away too. All our so-called Dad does is sleep. And day and night, all you do is worry. . . .*

Why do they shout so loudly?

Every part of the bug is linked with silence, but that's okay because to drive people away the bug need only make an appearance. I flopped down from the ceiling like a shepherd performing a miracle in the desert. The shock when they saw me made their minds go blank. Their hair turned white as paper. First sister, then mother, and then father, they ran like chickens. Just because you can't hear a bug's laugh doesn't mean they don't have a sense of humor.

The three family members driven out of their house gathered under the oblivion of their past lives. Like them, in my previous life, I was paralyzed by fear and besieged with coldness. But humans are animals that welcome the torture of hope. The family held a meeting to strategize. *We've isolated the bug. We've got to endure the difficulties and hunger until the bug starves to death. Only after the bug is dead can we die too.*

They're all dressed in underwear. Even the old man ran out of the bug's house in his knickers. *And as if things couldn't get worse, snow began to fall. Cold snow whitely covered our feet.*

* "I do not understand the 'scales of the world' and I'm sure they don't understand me any better (what could my 55 kilograms, undressed, begin to do with such monstrous scales; they wouldn't even notice, much less move)."—From Kafka's letter to Milena on Thursday, July 29, 1920

2

SUMMONING THE SOUL

You can't tell top from bottom
can't keep secrets like an echo
can't feel vertigo like a bird.
I love you.

I threw you into the river.
I scattered you into the air.

Rain at your front will turn to snow.
Snow at your back will turn to rain.

You can't tell front from back
can't tell sunlight from moonlight.
You don't know the way to me
but come to me from anywhere.
I love you.

DREAM WITHOUT SUBJECT

How do I dream the dreams you want?
Lifting and lowering my pillow like a wave. . . .
I want to dream your dreams.
All night I observe your sleeping face, studying it closely. . . .
I want to dig up . . . your face that you don't know.
If life slowly split us apart, death will hug us together.
As life doesn't know death, death doesn't know life.
How do I enter a seed again, be born again?
How do I take root elsewhere? As roots don't know their flowers,
flowers don't know their roots. They're far apart, like the distance
starlight travels between stars.
I put a hand on your heart. *Thump, thump, thump, thump.* . . .
On and on it moves toward me. The left foot appears while the right
vanishes, the right appears while the left vanishes, the left appears
while . . .
Thump, thump, thump . . . it's like a masked thief crossing like a bar
through a door while the village sleeps deep like a blizzard. On and on
it moves away.
A thief has to wait until the following night to return stolen goods.
Tomorrow, tomorrow. . . .
How do I climb over your wall and dream your unwanted dreams?
A fruit knife scrapes its way out of your throat. . . .
I want to taste the sweet liquid *drip, dripping.*

I wonder what fruit you peeled there. I want to dream your dreams.
Inside your dreams, I want to kill . . . my face that I don't know.
I want to peel . . . layer upon layer of red skin.
I'm always serious in my dreams. I never joke in my dreams.

UNFINISHED CLAY POT

I thought I raised you to make clay pots, but you've become someone who breaks them. Making a clay pot means shaping the inside and the outside. There must be an outside for the inside to exist. There must be an inside to step outside. My pot is beautiful on the outside and keeps secrets safe on the inside. There are moments when I pray for time to stop forever. They decide the form of the pot.

Clay pots are chaos. I thought I was inside, but I was abandoned outside. I thought I was outside, but I was trapped inside, crying for three days and nights. Well-wrought pots and unfinished pots break the same. When the illusion shatters, the pot disappears. To break a pot you must make it. To die you must be born. I fire the kiln and meditate on death, looming death. Aren't you inside the flames of death?

It seems I've raised you to break my pots. Are you trying to write with an ax? Your wrist tries to lift the ax, but the ax breaks your wrist. You fool—if you can't wield your weapon, your weapon will wield you. Speak! Who am I? You must know who I am before you can tell who you are.

If you make clay pots, I will break clay pots. Drinks ferment in some pots, while corpses rot in others. A snake slithers out of one pot, while a gun sinks into sticky silence in another. We always hesitated. I'm afraid to put my hand into the pot. I'm even more afraid to pull my hand out of the pot. Where's your hand? You don't understand your words, and I don't understand mine. It's impossible to tell who's speaking whose words, who's outside, who's inside.

But didn't you fail to finish a single pot? I ask again, who are you? If you know who you are, surely you can tell who I am.

THE FOOL'S TEMPERAMENT

Kent:	But who is with him?
Gentleman:	None but the fool; who labours to out-jest
	His heart-struck injuries.
	—Shakespeare, *King Lear*

Shakespeare: I hid my legacy in the fool's lines. Poet friend, study his words with care. The fool is always with us. He foretells tragedy with a face that seems not to know tragedy. He outruns us all, singing "hey ding a ding," and brings back stolen futures. My friend, I lived 400 years ago—how could I have known that the fool skipped to and fro between us? With a face that seemed not to know solitude, the fool opened his mouth like a coin purse because he was lonely. My friend, travel with the fool for the night. I like his jests. He shall make you laugh, even in a tragedy. However, the true nature of the laugh will reveal itself like red gums that outline those smiling white teeth. It will sink into the darkness like a man looking back, or a back that never looks back. If you seek the fool he is nowhere to be found, and he appears when you least expect him.

REFLECTIONS OF A HAIR ARTIST

Reflecting on life is like sailing up a long strand of hair as if it were the river of time. I never get seasick. If I spoke at the speed of growing hair, no one would understand me. So why are people afraid of hair? Hair doesn't work crawling on its hands and feet, it doesn't shut suffering out like eyelids. Hair isn't related to blood like the heart, it doesn't think, doesn't run, doesn't feel hunger, doesn't harbor hope. That's why hair is the most beautiful thing I own. I let beautiful things grow long and ripple as they like. "Mom, Mom, brush my hair." Thinking about my mother used to make me emotional. "Child, my child," she'd often climb onto my bed, jangling her scissors. Even in the maze of my dreams I dug tunnels and hid from her. She always said she'd lost her son.

In my youth, I worked at a small print shop. Letters turned into black rice in my dreams, and I stuffed them into my mouth. When they turned into bugs, I squashed them. The work wasn't hard, though it soaked me in sweat. I lost my job because of a book by Kafka. A single hair was printed on a page like a hostile country on a map. My boss said hair is what offends readers the most. He offensively wound my hair round and round on his fat finger like a bandage and said,

"Whose hair could this be?"

If I had to become the representative for all the hair in the world, I'd gladly be dragged before a crowd. Any man of legendary long hair can die for his hair, but it seems none of them are left. But if Kafka still lives . . . I'll keep on writing my story. I can be a hunger artist* by fasting and a hair artist by not cutting my hair. If I treat that fact like a forgotten dream, I could say I had friends. Everyone knows the hunger artist suffered because people doubted, tested, and forgot about his lack of appetite. It's not so well known that the spectators did not affect him. I want to write a letter to my friend and tell him about my dream.

Finally, I met a woman who tastes my hair like a snug blanket at night. In a tub full of my hair like a quilt in the laundry, we giggle and indulge in the pleasures of love. Don't sneer if I say our old love nest paid rent for our dreams. What kind of love doesn't wake from its dreams? I'll get married if the dream comes back. I'll write again.**

A nosy customer comes in. I should hide the letter. He visits regularly, holding a tape measure like a tailor. Hair length to him is like the height of a pole. Depending on his mood he either says life is long or laments how short it is. The man who drags me outside and cries "Behold the man!" forgets what comes next.

*Franz Kafka, A *Hunger Artist*, 1924.
**My friend remembers my letter someday in the future. I don't know why he included my confessions in his memoir. Since memories grow from forests of chaos, I can't blame him for his inaccuracies. In any case,

the part where my friend fondly remembers me is as follows. "At last my friend met a woman who finds hair as comfortable as a blanket, and he married her. He told me she washes his hair like a quilt. My friend became famous for his hair-growing feats. I can accept and appreciate the humor in other people's lives, but it's always harder for the choices I've made. When do happiness and misery grow apart like branches? While I hesitate, my black hair falls out and silver hair replaces it. If you ask what I've been doing lately, I've been using up the afternoon light to illuminate the past." (K., *Choices*, 2011.)

ON KAFKA'S BED

I woke up late for work. This has never happened before. I've gotten up with the alarm since my past life. If the hacking of the violent 6 a.m ax couldn't break the trunk of sleep I slumbered in, I wouldn't be surprised if someone snatched the trunk and departed the Earth with it. I must've been dead at 6 a.m, and that's why I wasn't surprised to wake up as a bug in Kafka's story.

Kafka tossed and turned because he poured his subconscious into writing instead of sleeping. His dreams and writing got mixed up. That's why he wasn't surprised when I woke up in his bed. *Yes. Let's say one morning Korean worker Kim woke up as a bug*, he muttered. His landlady came by to collect the overdue rent and heard his voice. *Tut tut, Kafka is talking to himself again.* From her perspective, Kafka was engaged in a silent argument with Kafka. This was seen as a bad sign. Someone who sleeps poorly, talks to himself, and writes about a man turning into a bug must be going mad. *I pity you Kafka, but you still need to pay rent.* As soon as she said that, a huge bug squirmed and flipped over on Kafka's bed. I lay chuckling, counting my extra legs. Many thin legs tickled the air.

Kafka, you also visited me. One time you left a black hat on the table like a secret code. And one night I was drafting a written apology when you burst in fretting you had to find your hat. I was tied up by your impatient gaze. Dreams are the perfect place to lose a key, and a door locks us in. Unless that door opens, we have to go round and round treading our shadows on the yellow linoleum floor like blind mole rats in the sun. Over a long time, it feels like my tongue and ears have slowly worn out. I left my umbrella in the office and you left your hat. It was raining when I came out of the railway station. I thought about my umbrella in the rain. Why Kafka were you so anxious to find your hat that night?

They say you can't tickle yourself. But there are moments when I'm not me and Kafka is not Kafka. If we must continue laughing *hahaha*, we'll finally sink into unbearable pain. I must flip myself. Many thin legs are laughing at the air. Clamoring. *Hey, help me. Kafka, Kafka. What are you looking at? What are you listening to?* Kafka dives into writing like he's being chased.

THE UNSLEEPING EAR

1

Hi, I'm the ear that clings to you like a shade on a summer's day. Even when you're fast asleep, I listen to your breathing, your snoring. A North Korean anchor suddenly raises her voice from the TV you leave on all night. All these are vibrations of air. A bell rings somewhere. Who rings a bell at this late hour? I want to shake you out of sleep like a tidal wave.

2

Your old mother came to your room one day, lamenting some young woman's foolishness from 40 years ago. She had beauty but didn't know how to use it to her advantage. *Sleep tight, my poor baby.* These are all arrows. You pretended to be asleep. I heard your breathing, your muffled scream, and the sound of an old woman crying with her entire face. I understood your silence that day. You couldn't speak, just like me. I hoped all this would pass. And then, one day, she died.

3

Someone must be beating their chest somewhere, and someone somewhere must be pounding a wall until their fist breaks. Sounds I can't hear are ringing in the air somewhere. I imagine sounds you can hear that I can't. In my dreams you devour me. I want to swallow you up like a high tide. Water *drip, drips* from the tap. All these sounds are collisions of air. All these are collisions of planets. The wall-pounding person wants to make a certain someone stand up against the wall, and that's why they tear their skin and bleed, bleed, bleed. All these fragments.

4

And one day, I find you talking to yourself. Talking to yourself and thinking to yourself, are they the same? If I can't be your talking partner, I'll be your secret. I'll grow bigger in secret. One day, with you in my arms, I'll silently explode.

THE EMOTION OF EVENING

It's like making the lowest body.

It's like crouching in front of a growling dog and saying tearfully,
there, there.

It's like creating a lower social class.
It's like trying to get up and feeling faint from anemia.

It's like vertigo surging like an emotion and becoming a sob. How do
waves return?

On a beach where people go missing
 and only their black swim tubes return . . . . Like a slanting cursive

It's like lying down and feeling your back dampen.

If you don't close your eyes,
it's like believing the deafening sound in the sky is tonight's first star.

If you close your eyes,
it's like patting yourself on the back for closing your eyes.

It's like returning as the second verse.

THE STAIRCASE OF NIGHT

A deep night is three people looking at the moon on a small apartment rooftop. Two people think they're all alone because one person can't be told apart from the darkness.

An even deeper night is made of cubicles that make up offices and offices that make up a building that becomes one empty box. Like a magic trick that whisks people away into a different world . . . and then whisks them back, someone walks out of the huge, square labyrinth like a black matchstick. The flames that fiercely snapped at that person's body, where have they gone?

The deepest night is the moon's gravity that pulls the staircase into the sky like tidal waves. It means that the person foundering in the staircase is overwhelmed to find how deep the bottom of life is.

THE EXISTENCE OF GLASS

Palms on the window, I touch what I can't pass through. . . . And I finally feel like I can wake up from the dream. So the invisible walls were the glass's conspiracy.

That's why I shattered when I fell. That's why I bled when I held you.

Removing my palms from the window, I thought, *staring straight like dark eyes at the world made up of things I can't touch—isn't that how the dead stare at the living?* Glass never makes a face. The handprints left on glass don't belong to it.

The faint breath that remains on the glass will soon vanish. Throw rocks at me. Please. Or else I'll throw them myself. I feel like I'll do something soon, real soon. I finally feel the existence of the glass I'd worn all this time like layers of death.

Sunlight comes pouring through the glass like a miracle. You stand outside the window. But whenever you shine down like sunlight, I'm the one standing outside the window.

COFFEE AND UMBRELLA

"He left his umbrella. He's always absent-minded. But he says he gets up on the scale and checks his weight with a serious face almost every day. Whether you lose a bit or gain a bit, the weight of flesh is solid proof that you exist." That's why we pinch our skin.

"*Coffee and Cigarettes* is a real classic. Famous actors made cameos. Everything feels like a coincidence when a familiar face flashes on screen. A cup of coffee, two cigarettes. That's all I ever needed. Those days when we used to smoke at coffee shops are history." So nostalgia is like what a ghost feels.

These clear plastic umbrellas are see-through and light. They're perfect for a ghost's hand. Ghosts must also get wet from the rain. "Umbrellas can be bought for the price of a coffee or a pack of cigarettes. Umbrellas and coffee and cigarettes all go pretty well with rain."

"Can you trade this coffee for an umbrella at the convenience store across the street? Can you bite and suck on an umbrella, light it up, and puff it up in smoke? If you can't, why do umbrellas and coffee and cigarettes all cost the same? In the end, you can only choose one." Do you know what I had to give up to keep that one thing? This world.

He returned to the coffee shop. What did you have to lose to find the umbrella? You hold on tight to this one plastic umbrella—who abandoned you? "If I got rained on today, I'd really want to die." The rain stopped. But it feels like raindrops are about to fall, right? The color of the sky, the color in your face . . .

UMBRELLA AND CIGARETTES

Just then the storm turned into an old man crossing the skies of Seoul.
He said he was going north.
If you were looking up at the sky,
you might've seen that silver-haired old man.
There's always something above our heads.
Hats, umbrellas, ashy clouds, cathedral roofs,
beach parasols, starlit skies. . . . And time is always passing.
When you burst out laughing,
when that sound alone filled up your lungs
when the hat also twirled in the air
and spun down like the sound of laughter
when I happened to pass by and picked up your hat
when I talked to you for the first time. . . .
The story that begins with "when"
runs toward us like the light of time from the past.
Hats and umbrellas are good for losing.
Clouds are good for losing too, so
when I look at the sky after lighting a cigarette,
it's cloudless and clear.
Then I want to change the subject.
The story that begins with "when" shines future light and leads me
like a donkey in the morning to a place where I don't exist.
15 years in the future,
a place where a thrifty person uses the umbrella I lose.
As always, it rains softly.
As always,
cigarette smoke slowly spreads out from under your black umbrella.

THE CHIMNEY SWEEP IS HERE

"Well, we don't have a chimney here. . . ."

But your face is dark with soot, you're like what's left of a tree after it burnt, and you smell smoky. There's a famous story about chimney sweeps. Two angels came down to this world after cleaning chimneys. One of them was covered in soot while the other was spotless. The angel with the clean face ran to the well to wash its face. The hard-sweeping angel smiled a sooty smile and went to clean another chimney. That dark angel became a dark spot in this universe. This story is only possible when two people face each other. So let's talk.

"There's a Jewish saying that goes, 'When a miller fights with a chimney sweep, the miller gets black and the chimney sweep gets white.' Does it mean we should fight? Not fight?"

Do what you want.

"If the miller and the chimney sweep shake hands after a big fight, then whose hand is black and whose is white?"

There's another story where the miller and the chimney sweep fall in love and write love letters with flour and soot. Stories birth stories and dreams birth dreams. Instead of dreaming your dreams, why don't you come sweep chimneys with me? Hey you, Walking Chimney, ever heard the wise words inscribed on a pillar, "Know thyself?" Your house is made of fire and smoke and coughs. Smoke is the gesture of the visible that wants to become the invisible. It's the most beautiful movement. You know, I loved stopping at the garden after work to stare vacantly at the smoke escaping your chimney. All the world's smoke is infused with sadness, but to me, it means you aren't cold. And now you've filled the chimney like it was a well. In any case, now that the chimney is found, there'll be a way.

"Last night I listened to some drunks endlessly ramble and then I passed out as if I was buried in a large, black liquor jar. In the backyard of the alcohol rehab center sat a man who fell in a well in his youth and a former chimney sweep who broke her leg after falling from a chimney that she climbed while holding an alcohol bottle. They talked and talked and talked, their hands trembling.* The boys who climbed out of the deep well of their childhood still shout, 'Don't stop.'"

"Don't stop." That's what you tell yourself. Stories mix with stories, as you go deeper into the story it catches fire, and as you silently watch the things that burn, you realize there's no escape. Outside the door, the chimney sweep is already here.

*Raymond Carver, "Where I'm Calling From"

GREGOR SAMSA'S DAY OFF

A single mirror hung on the bare wall across from the bed of the man who woke up as a bug the next morning. "Finally, tomorrow's my day off, so I'll sleep a sleep longer than death. Gregor Samsa, Gregor Samsa. I like mumbling your name, it feels somniferous." The woman who lay next to him vanished. Where'd she go? The happy woman who chanted "Gregor, Gregor" last night, where'd she go?

Gregor Samsa sleeping with a woman was, you know, unusual. But he was, you know, familiar with the waking up alone part. But that woman last night who mentioned sleep longer than death—her disappearance felt like, you know, crossing over to the other side. So then, where on earth is this place?! Gregor Samsa felt like he could choke himself.

He appeared to stare into the mirror, but Gregor Samsa was actually looking at things the mirror didn't show. He only had dinner with her twice but learned that she takes the same train to work at the same time every day. So each morning between 6:20 and 6:25 he stared at people outside the station. Those people he stared at, those people he knew weren't her, whose only defining quality was that they weren't her. Those non-distinct, unmemorable people. Why did he recall those faces from the crowd? Who did those faces belong to? The mirror on the opposite wall showed a bug.

Hey, this is my face! I know, I know it well. This is surely the face I made all night. Today is just another day. But she's gone and I have a giant day off. And I've no reason to run to the train station, no matter how many feet I have. "Gregor Samsa, Gregor Samsa." If I mumble my name with her voice, I could sleep a deep sleep, but . . . my love has left, and now my name is of no use.

CIGARETTES AND CONTE

Let me tell you a story. A story as short as the dagger you carry. A story like ash from a slow-burning cigarette, ash that can't return to the fire. It was a rainy day like today, a good day to talk to myself.

An umbrella floated midair like a leaf that fell on dirty water. It looked like a question mark drawn in the air. The person holding the umbrella was unseen, just like what's under the surface of water is unseen. W-w-was that who drowned last night?

I rubbed my eyes as if rubbing out a cigarette. Not that I could kill my old eyes and get new ones. Two eyes stabbing in different directions like two branches branching off midair.

At first, I thought I had to defeat that apparition. I'm sure my eyes flickered like the horrifying ideas that woke me. *I made up that umbrella I see. I'll take that umbrella from the ghost's hand and throw it to the ground. I can't live in this world if I have to follow this ghost.* I hurried on. I almost ran. I finally jumped into the umbrella and became as light as someone who jumped into a dream. I bounced off like a water drop. My goodness, it didn't hurt a single bit. Did the umbrella pole hanging upside-down in midair shake a little? The person who caught my body was an old man. I thought he shivered a bit, but that was it. Shivering to an old man is like a slight cough. It's like a dry cough. He had the energy to walk, and the passengers on this street all reeked of staleness and rugged melancholy. "Strong people, oh strong people. Oh, those of you with strength left in your body." This voice that can't stop a single person felt sad for some reason. I mumbled and went out like a cigarette butt.

All the same, I was dreaming a different dream. Like having one eye open and one eye closed—that's to say, like a wink sent to a lovely being. *I want to protect that apparition. I want to stand like a fence outside the boundaries of that apparition, my arms wide open. I want to stand with my arms round and wide open, for my lover is finally running toward me.* "Just the thought makes me happy," I mumbled, when surprisingly, the umbrella walked toward me with the footsteps of the moon and clouds and dogs. The umbrella with an empty bottom was heartbreakingly painful. Oh, now that I'm in love with something I can't touch, I can't touch what I love. The umbrella is passing me—you are passing me. Since our time together under the umbrella is so short, do not pass away!* The umbrella passes me like a ghost. . . . Oh, you don't even recognize me. When I look back, you're already walking away with the umbrella in your hand. A dog tags along, getting drenched in the rain. The leash is loose, and I've lost it somewhere. I've lost it all. Walking with a black rock-like backpack, you flick your cigarette butt away, *HWEEK*, as if whistling. Beautiful moment,* you're like a cigarette's flame, not yet dead, flickering in the air like a firefly.

*"Beautiful moment, do not pass away!" (Goethe, *Faust*)

3

THE SCULPTURE GARDEN

A pigeon is sticking its beak between its toes in, out, in, like a pendulum. I saw its name, "Untitled II," beside its toes. The time was—nod, nod—passing.

A woman stood at its side, brushing the grass with the palms of her hands. Whenever her palm slowly moved, the grass changed the direction of its body to obey. I couldn't tell what she was thinking.

THE GOODBYE ABILITY

I am all the things that take gaseous form.
I am cigarette smoke for 2 minutes.
I am rising steam for 3 minutes.
I am oxygen entering your lungs.
I will gladly burn you away.
Did you know there is smoke billowing from your head?
The meat fat you hate is gently burning
and the intestines became an exhaust pipe
and the blood boils
and all the birds in the world leave to immigrate
commanding all the world's fog and

I sing for more than 2 hours
do the laundry for more than 3 hours
nap for more than 2 hours
meditate for over 3 hours
and of course, I see the apparitions. They are super beautiful.
I love you for more than 2 hours and

I love the things that exploded out of your head.
Birds snatched the bawling children
and took them away.
I learned that in the middle of doing eternal laundry.
My coat turned into gas.
I pulled a cloud out of my pocket. Your cane.

Well, that's that. In the middle of singing an endless song
in the middle of taking an endless nap

there were moments I opened my eyes.
When my eyes and ears get clear,
and my Goodbye Ability peaks,
I shed my fur, and I am cigarette smoke for 2 minutes.
Rising steam for 3 minutes.
The smell disappears for 2 minutes.
I take off my clothes. To the clothes
dispersing into the distant horizon
to my neighbors
I wave.

PEOPLE BELOW THE DECIMAL POINT

Third Visit

If 0.4 were a cloud, he'd bark woof woof like a good dog, like a person with a terribly bad memory. "Nice to meet you," 0.4 says and I realize I've come to see him. I confess, he erases. I lose something important as if I'm about to fall asleep.

Our Promise

Because my twin brother 0.5 made a promise in my name, I became a traitor. Feeling wronged, I grabbed his collar and we brawled, but unable to tell who was who, I soon ran out of energy. Oh, the fist that came flying and the identical face behind it! As I got beaten, I denied you three times and accepted you six times before feeling brotherly love. And even so, we'll disagree to the very end.

Towards 0.0

they each walked. The time of the day was always getting bright or getting dark.

Nursing Home Windows

0.8 is the nursing home windows. Patients learn the meaning of nursing through these windows. The windows of day show nearby flower trees and faraway seas. B.B. is a young lady, around 20, who's come to nurse her heart. Her fast-beating heart, on the verge of bursting, arrived first at the doorstep. Many bombs are buried under the thin blankets of the nursing home. They wander the hallways and pick flowers in the garden. When nearby flower trees grow far and faraway seas grow near, it's nighttime for the windows. When ears get soaked in the rolling waves of the nearby and faraway seas, you can watch people walk on water. B.B. strolled along the beach each night. Even as she walked, nearby seas were near, and faraway seas were far.

The Face of the Beach
Melting, forever approaching, boiling, buzzing,

0.01
The following morning, 0.01 was lying on the street. 0.01 was a slanted man, so the sight of him gave me comfort. I squatted down. Like a child playing with dirt, I gathered 0.01, sprinkled fine bits of him, and dug deep. A shape like an underpass formed. I reached in, pulled out, reached in,

LIKE MUSIC

This winter, on a snowy sofa with a rabbit,
I sat on the floor with a quiet friend,
listened to music *largo*,
dug a tunnel,

ate lunch *andante*,
dug a tunnel,
and met the dead. Past those quiet people

we dug on
and went a little farther.
Next day was the same,

the tunnel made time pass like a novel,
and we didn't speak.
On the snowy sofa, I yarned, *andante, andante*.
A pair of clothes melted softly.

A WORLD OF KINDNESS

Here, my feet melt.
Knees disappearing, I don't ever want to get up from here.

It's alright, a small voice becomes even smaller.
We dim together.

Thank you, with those round lips
we gestured patterns used to say goodbye.
So long, one ear turns transparent at those words.

When a black dolphin emerges from
a world lying like a horizon

when our knees shine
we get closer, arms open wide.

FASCINATION FOR WINDOWS

I told you the reason I came here so often was because of the giant windows. The number of stars we see in the night sky increases as the quality of telescopes improves.

What? The sudden rise in coffee shops in the neighborhood is due to giant windows? To the youth of a hundred years ago, glass windows were a modern and mysterious object. For the last one hundred years, kids have been scolded for breaking windows in every alley in the world. I think it's all the same whether we have windows or not.

When you said it was all the same, you had the most naive look on your face. You idiot, as the bright coffee shop windows push back the night, the darkness takes your face away as a reflection in the mirror.

I drink coffee as I study. My goal is to pass the exam and become a civil servant. One who finishes work at 6 p.m. sharp.

I can witness the 6 o'clock magic from where I'm sitting. The astonishing spectacle . . . one by one, light bulbs hanging from second-floor ceilings inside coffee shops line up in the space behind windows. When I look at the light bulbs hanging in the blue sky at 8 in the evening . . . one by one, I somehow feel like I'm losing friends. Behind their windows.

I think people have loved windows for at least a hundred years. A white bird is seen flying through a coffee house window. Two people, one who thinks the window is fake, and one who thinks the bird is fake, sit facing each other. They sip their coffees.

KISS IN THE FOREST

When two necks
like two pillars, create a house, a space
when windows open
hands fly like bursting fireworks.
Two people stand like trees.
Trees walk like people, walk fast.
Two necks lean forward.
The kiss is soft.
A water drop softly abandons its leaf, drops bigger.
Set off the scent of the forest.
Two necks put on each other's faces.
My face sprouts from your neck

HORMONOGRAPHY

O Hormone, light me morning-bright. The rage is swelling, and I want to manifest it like the eye of a typhoon. That man cheated me. I shall hunt him to the end.

Through your milk-lines, I flow to you, I am river Soyang, I am river Nakdong. I am a boatman without an oar. Wherever I end up, if you call me as a man, as a man I will. . . .

If you call me as a woman, I'll immerse myself in womanhood. From the third, fourth, and seventh rung of the ladder between heaven and hell, I'll caress the cards dealt to me until I'm destitute. Exhaust me. O Hormone, with the gentle caress of your hand, lower the lids of my eyes and

stir up my dreams. I'll be your movie theater. O Hormone, through big waves stir the landscapes and facial expressions until the screen goes black, until we reach a war-like meaninglessness.

At the mountain spring of the holy hormone
signals twinkle eternally.

SANTA SANGRE

—This amount of blood could save at least three people.
—You only care about the quantity of things. This volume of
blood from a nosebleed is impressive, but blood is useless in
this age when all holy superstitions have disappeared.
—from Jodorowsky's *Santa Sangre*

Within the elephant bleeding out of her trunk
there is a baby elephant who is pumping out her blood.
In the outside world, what kind of manual labor do people do to reach death?
Mother, I will labor myself to death in my heaven.

The elephant's ears flap. Her enormous body gets baggy.
Mother, we are cleaning together. Your trunk makes a great hose.
Come on, perk up, and spray all around us.

The elephant's blood creates a colosseum.
The audience is gathered by the blood.
Our death battles are headed in the same direction, so we are at peace.
But, mother, I am still afraid of their orgasms.

Now the elephant's skin drapes saggily. The skeleton supporting the appearance of the elephant is triumphant.

Mother, it is empty here. I'm a little cold and hungry, but I enjoyed the labor. Mother, this place right here, it is still my heaven.*

*This image comes from a scene in Alejandro Jodorowsky's film *Sante Sangre* where a collapsed elephant continues to spurt blood from its trunk.

MR. CAT'S APPRENTICESHIP

It's not like my eyes shone the first night I left home determined to become a cat. Ever since I was 13, I've wanted lonely eyeballs, but I could only roll them till they lost focus. I wish someone would've kicked them for me.

A cat draws an arc in the sky as it flies. Ah, I wanted to lie in a grassy field like that.

Nights are long and naps are sweet. She's carrying six kittens. She was my teacher and my lover. *Annyeong*, Lala. A cat's path often forks. It's like six kittens. *Annyeong*, Mimi.

When I first confessed that I would become a cat, my brother whispered kindly in my ear. "You've always been a kitten. Once you crawled out from under your blanket, all the little rats under this roof vanished. Think about Mom and Dad. What on earth happened?" My brother was my missionary.

He became a black-suited crook, and I began shedding again. Ah, so light and soft. I think my fur will be thicker and cozier this winter.

Now I walk the long path of the cat. Every quiet night, I practice yowling. It's a cat thing. Like moonlight, like wind howling, I'll never know what I'm saying.

FRANKENSTEIN'S BRIDE

I was born in a lab. In my fluorescent blue sleeping bag, I stretched—
"*ahhh*"–and blinked my eyes like filaments. "Doctor, Doctor, please
make more waves. Please make me feel."

I was born in a lab. Doctor says "Good morning," commemorating the
day as he gives me a kiss. He says today is the early 18th century, and
tomorrow is the late 21st.

My love is a cyborg who issued a suicide proclamation, and I was
born in a lab to adore his lofty mind. "The white mice are growing
awfully fat, Doctor, Doctor, do you think they can pull our carriage
tomorrow?"

Today is the early 18th century, and the love of my life walks with his
dirty cloak flapping, so alone. Tomorrow is the late 21st century and
our wedding.

"Doctor, Doctor, does nobody experiment outside of the lab?"
Since I was born in a lab, instead of a first cry I had a first love, my
Frankenstein. "Goodbye, goodbye," Doctor will say, blessing my
future.

My chest is still small, but from earth to sky, *thump.*

72 WAYS TO TAKE A WALK

Walking as if following someone in secret
is one way.
From one method comes a four-, then a five-way intersection.
Seems like a stream of people will pour out.
I saw a dog, too.

Would a dog turn around
and bark, "Why?"
Would the dog think of our connection?

Walking while thinking of my connection to the dog is another way.
Today I walked as if following someone
and thought of the closed door behind him.
I thought of the closed door in front of me.
It would've been very sad if I . . . loved him.

And if I . . . didn't know him
I would've been exposed by irrational sadness.
"What're you doing here?"

Mulling over 72 ways of taking a walk is one way, but
burning the left side of your face red like the west sky
as sunlight tilts
until it lies down in a perfect line
is another.

A MYSTERY

People who sleep by day
people who sleep at night
when do they meet?

The times people meet are a mystery.
Even those who sleep both day and night have places to be.

12 o'clock
13 o'clock

My shadow also talks of time.
Now I grow longer.
How far? Now I'm walking.

Closer than when
people who sleep by day and
people who sleep at night
meet

people walk, looking only ahead.
The backs of their heads are black, pitch black.
Who are they?

FEET

There are men with ugly feet. But beautiful, overall. My dancers.
My pride.

Energy gathers at their toes. I think of their tendons when I pray.

They're long. When falling, their hands are furthest from their feet.

HANDS

When the horses get separated from the carriage
the carriage doesn't *stop!*
The carriage
doesn't stop and think.

I don't think,
I write, like hooves galloping away from me.

Like characters collapsing dramatically in the finale
like the actress rising again, beaming as she takes a bow
like someone else.

Like the whip curving midair
I touched
and loved.

I write. After writing, I write without erasing.

I pass the murder scene, the dropped knife, the twice-dropped hand,
the rake, my poverty.
Like the pursuer's touch
I become bright
and persistent.

The king makes a fist.
Bang! He strikes the round table's center, and
as my wings rise,
dice drop on the world.

THE POSITION OF THE NECK

Isn't it odd? The head's position.

I crook my neck to say hello. I bend my neck back and look up at the night sky. Right after greeting you, if the neck immediately cranes to the ceiling or night sky, it is a kind of neck that reveals only a single line of movement. And this means, once again, my mind was made to track the traces of my neck. Like rushing to pick up and put on clothes because of shame.

To avoid your eyes, which direction must the neck avoid, and which direction must the neck stop in again? The night sky, isn't it confusing? The shape of the neck.

Aren't I vague? About you.

A cough popped out of my neck. Suddenly I remembered the writing of some epicure that read *I want to have the longest throat in the world.* Does the ecstasy that food gives sink more slowly the longer the neck is? Or does the sight of the food slowly departing stretch the pain thinner and thinner? Or are we just in the middle of carefully whittling down the white bones of happiness until they finally fall apart? Suddenly everything here disappears.

It's no use—adjusting the length of the neck. Making the neck disappear into a coat. It's still cold and impossible. Hiding the large frame of the body.

Even so, isn't there something I want to accomplish—accomplish by moving my neck? Like moving my legs to leave you. Like moving my legs to find you again.

ROADSIDE TREE CARETAKERS

Good people

Most good people are shy the first time you meet them. "Hello." They talk about the weather. It can't be said that the weather isn't personal. It tells you a lot when you become sensitive to it. So I met a roadside tree caretaker and knew she was a good person. She was in charge of 8th Street. How elegantly did the trees of 8th Street drop their leaves, and how sadly did they sprout new ones? I understand the person who plans to jump off a building because of a single leaf. I carefully hid my jealousy, but the caretaker praised me for it. We became friends. Our friendship didn't just transcend age. Trust transcended trust and made many things possible.

Hey, do me a favor

Tonight, the sky is the most transparent I've ever seen it. The weather is very personal. What use is it to say that life is like a well or the sea? Every time we're swept up in personal weather, we dream of a unique day.

Do me a favor. Let me sleep on your tree for the night. Tonight won't deepen easily. Why do we become nauseous, and why are we bent on heading home? We're familiar with the last group to leave the bar on 8th Street. If the vulgarity of insults had magical powers, we'd all be dead by now. But the bed is magical tonight. I'll rise like a quiet flame and walk up the branches of the tree on 8th street until I'm soaked in moonlight. I'll meet people who can't sleep. I won't write a single line to describe the face that captivated them. What use is it? Tonight is the only transparent night.

Hey, do me a favor. Tonight is the only transcendent night. Your tree is our bed tonight. Let's invite all the beggars on 8th Street!

The 13th Street roadside tree caretaker

The trees on 13th Street are cared for by the 13th Street roadside tree caretaker. Everyone knows he has the most beautiful hands. He's been in bed for a month with a fever. A black dog keeps vigil at his side, licking his hot forehead with her long, long tongue. The trees on 13th Street haven't dropped a leaf for a month. Perhaps their will, unswayed by strong gusts of wind, belongs to the black dog. A strong spirit flows like an epidemic. Children shine in the sun like Jonathan apples and bloom like frogs as they hop over walls. The people of 13th Street feared the trees on 13th Street for the first time. During that month, trees became the theme of nightmares. People bade each other "good night" with darkening faces before parting ways.

The good-bye ability

They're old people. They gaze at the horizon and feel the world that includes us. The 13th Street roadside tree caretaker died, leaving the black dog behind. The 14th Street roadside tree caretaker keeps Death seated by his side and makes small talk that could be stopped at any time. Chairs creak. The horizon moves quickly. People walk around. The shops on 8th Street open, and clerks busily rearrange items or dust them off. Today I'm meeting you for the first time. "Nice morning, huh?" We examine the weather. A young man eating breakfast on the tree laughed. Grains of rice scattered with laughter. Chirping birds flew after them.

4

THE CHORUS

You're the stage, as long as we follow you. You're a little short of faith.
When your words start to slow into a blur,
we open up like the lips of Heaven. Take a step back, my love. That's
a cliff you're standing on. The bored-to-death spectators open their
mouths so wide they could rip. Take a step back and stretch. After that
lonely exercise, stand in front of us and sing like you could fly, sing like
you could fall. You're the stage, as long as we follow you.
You can lower the curtains whenever you want. My love, you carry a
few chairs behind the curtains, and we add sequins to our long dresses.
You contribute to beauty. You're the stage, as long as we follow you.
Although you're a little short of faith,
you know how to face straight. You know how to see nothing.

CO-EVOLVING COUPLES

When you offer your hand the dance begins.
"The birth of a new couple!"— Some people talk like spectators.
But even when they're furthest apart
couples run toward each other for a hug.
Something impossible when you're alone.
That's why we do things together, even fights.
Your hand enters your pocket,
my hand enters mine.
What if I wore clothes without pockets?
Aha! The black pocket is important. Thinking alone in the dark.
Something impossible as a couple:
Talking to yourself.

When hands and feet first became distinct
how did the hands feel?
What was it like to float mid-air?
Whose hand was hidden in the darkness? A match lights up.
When shadows take on color
unpredictable things jump out.
When two hands first split left and right
when something you pretended not to know
really becomes unfathomable
like an eternal riddle
love keeps answering, "I love you."
And even if I hate you, the story goes on.

THE LOCATION OF BIRDS

How heavy are birds that take flight? How much weight defies gravity?
Let's love lightly. I'm in a good mood,
so I'll lose to you today, lose to you tomorrow.
Aww, it's snowing. Feathers stick to my coat, and
birds dying mid-air don't defy gravity.
We're as silent as dead birds.
I want to hug you like air.
My arm will loosen and fall off, my leg will loosen and fall off.
I want to spill myself wherever I go.
I can't "be careful," I can't "try harder."
Today feels like it's yesterday morning,
like it's yesterday afternoon, and
it's snowing. So many things can't be done,
but today is great for forming footprints.
Everyone's busy making them. "So cold,"
they repeat and walk around staring at the ground.
Snow falls silently but crunches when you step on it.
Let's talk like falling snow. I speak to you like an inaudible sound.
Speak like a dead bird
and walk away petting the corpse of a bird in my hands.

THE EXISTENCE OF BIRDS

Beings with feet of differing height
instantly making and
destroying stairs

like creatures with thousands of feet
everywhere
at every moment
like the place where new music begins

you kill them by pressing on their hearts.*
No matter whose heart it is
the distance to it
is closer than couples who confuse love and death.

Someone crossed a nondescript field in a snowstorm and lost feeling
in their feet.
When the snow and ice-covered ground sinks
like the foot that
presses on the snow and
smashes the ice's blue flesh
the bird's heart

flies off
by pressing on the air.

*Peter Hoeg, *Smilla's Sense of Snow*

EMBRACE

Closer, until we can't see each other. Did I fade to black? You're very close.

Closer, until I can't see you. To where we break like a wave engulfing a wave. What does "we" mean when we're that close?

Until we become lovers who can't see each other till the end of time.

We overlap. Like two lips achieving silence. Like the mouth of a time about to unravel.

THE BED SAYS

I haven't lost the qualities that make me a bed. My little squeaking sounds are also part of me. It's your problem if you feel like you're lying on top of a cutting board. You scream as if your feet were cut off like scallion roots. Isn't that because you don't want to leave me? Really, really, in this moment, do you empathize with a scallion's pain?

Why do you come to me with all your problems? Today, you lie down like a kitchen knife. A bed can put a kitchen knife to sleep like it can your lover or child. Are you mincing and chopping on me? Raising your arm and striking it down? Your bed is always there to connect everything smoothly. I remember your arm connecting to your pen, which connected to your notebook, which connected to long stories, which connected to endless nights. I want to connect the dreams you began in the morning and connected to the brightest hour of the day.

It's your problem if you feel like you're lying on a mirror. You think you have the bed all to yourself. You ignore the bed's memory. Can you imagine what unfolded on top of me? You think a bedsheet can erase it all. I remember the meaningless syllables the dying person uttered when they died. Is what they failed to put together a single word? The first syllable received potential from the lips of death and the next syllable broke off and ran far away like light. First, it became an infinite sentence and then a letter, neverending like space. I remember his feces and urine and the love of his final years. The memory of the pair of bodies making love reaches deep into my fluff. Like when humans, requiring sleep, dig into the earth for a place to lie down for a final rest, OOHH, appearing to lick death, humans crave, despise, lust, and cry out for another body, becoming the loneliest they've ever been. There's no "stop" in the lexicon of sleep. Sleep is like a flame that heats up and AH! scorches your asses. As though staring at a night sky in perpetual motion, I can sketch the moments deepening like a cave, moments of the flesh that had long rested inside of me and that I had grown attached to. You all sink deeper like a bedsore that tormented the little body and rose to magnificence during sleep. Why do you look away?

Why do you roll to your side like you saw something you couldn't bear? It's like you're performing a one-man play. Who wrote your script? Am I the stage? Or am I the audience sitting with arms crossed in the dark? It's your problem which side you choose to lie on. That's today's solitude.

A bed doesn't care about human whims. I'm with you whenever, wherever. You're always exhausted because you're a wimp. What you truly want is to submit to sleep. Follow with your eyes closed to wherever. Color yourself head to toe in the dye of sleep. All night long, I help you in your struggle. Whether on top of a cutting board, a mirror, or a clock's pointed hand, sleep will find you.

RESIDENTIAL STREET

What's a home?
What's childhood?
I recall my 20th-century childhood
and you recall your 21st-century childhood.
That's what a residential street is like these days.
Just like the rules at your mom's house
and the rules at your dad's house
everyone goes about life differently
though they want to look the same.

People with big dogs depend on their big dogs
and people with small dogs depend on their small dogs.
There must be someone crying with a dog smaller than their head
wrapped tightly in their arms.
Tonight too, that's what a residential street is like.
A dog squirms.
Does it mean it's happy, or distressed?
If it was a talking dog, would it bark the truth?
If it was a talking window, it would be a talkative grandma.
But even if it was a kind-hearted grandma
you couldn't continue your monologue by the window.
What does it mean to escape a residential street at night?

I envy the speed at which cars race toward
the gas station at night.

You walk out of the alley and jump into an alley-less world.
What changes like an illusion?
What do we believe firmly like a perfect illusion?
The night breeze is cool, so I close the windows.
I close the see-through glass window
and the opaque glass window
shutting the curtains, as if angry.
I can't see either.

VANISHING STAIRCASE

I confess through a snake. I can borrow a snake's shape
but not its nature.

A snake coils itself up you. It feels good.
Speaking of the snake, you're a staircase.

The snake's shape is a staircase, but no one thinks to walk up a snake.
If you did, the staircase would slither away and vanish halfway up.

So I borrowed the snake briefly
and began my walk past 3 in the afternoon.

CHOCOLATE GRINDER

> I understood through life
> the need for constant rotation.
> By rotating around its axis, this machine
> somehow manages to produce chocolate.
> —Duchamp

It's your lullaby
your fine powdered medicine.
It puts you to sleep.

It begins slowly.
Like soft chocolate
showing rotten teeth.
It's surprising they can bite.
Mothers.
Sisters.
These kinds of women.

You can't tell chocolate from the night sky
the sound of screaming gets finely ground.
Without a word
the machine produces.
Mothers.
Sisters.

I want to fall asleep to their lullabies.
You've grown into an adult.

It began slowly.
On top of an aluminum disc.

GUARDIAN

Rain separates inside from outside. I want to talk inside the rainstorm's effects. The black water in the teacup is silent. It's a beautiful teacup. But I'm an easily breakable pot. A pricey one, but oh well. What's one pot? Your father is a rich merchant. Don't fuss, stay in me like black water. Stay in me till your death.

Like the line of pine trees bending over the beach, I stretch my long arms toward you. But you look around to make sure you're alone. The feeling of being watched—it seems to torture you. I exist for you as an eyeball. I exist for you as a tape recorder that winds and winds. I display you, play you, I'm almost you. It's a bad habit to dig deep into the heart. Don't shut me out. Even if it's a lie, it's alright, go on, keep lying. I'll pretend to believe and then believe. If lips don't call out the heart, the endlessly flaming heart will burn the lips. I call that the devil. I want to wait for you in your future.

I'll guide you into your future. You must've seen the devil. I call that a dream. Did you run desperately like a scream? My panting love, my baby, whose opposite side did you wake up on? I'll clean up the dream shards. Don't touch them, don't. . . . Oh, this is my blood. It's real blood. Don't mind it. Because we're one. You no longer see yourself, you only see me. Right? Right?

BLADE
— Adolescence 3

The boy opens his hand. There's a blade. Blood oozes from his pink palm. "Why don't you sharpen a pencil." The girl visibly scoffs. She fixes her eyes at the boy.

Has a girl ever comforted me? The boy can't recall. He's scared of the girl who's never scared. The boy's never been to her house. He's never invited her over. But he likes dreaming

about piling hot sand on the girl's round breasts as she lies on the beach. Birthday parties are for rich schoolkids. "You wouldn't open your palm to anyone, would you?" The girl is smart.

The boy grins and slowly closes his palm. The blade vanishes. So do his fingers.

UNFINISHED SYMPHONY

I'll show you on the field trip.
Just chill out.
I like you.

Isn't it refreshing?
This building's windows are open like crazy.
The stairs end in midair.
The building laughs.
I like you.
Bird droppings drip.
Boys come to fight.
Someone made a fire here.
There's no second floor.
There's no self.
In the halls, we'll unwrap our food

and spread the smell.
I'll show you on the field trip.
The building smiled.

Let's exit out the back.
Let's vanish together.
Like music.

FOR WHOM THE BELL TOLLS

I gather my hands in the evening.
One day my hands feel hot.
They seem to shake as if they hold a gun.

Once the illusion of a gun vanishes
only the hand remains
like a black bird that got shot.

For no reason
the toy roly-poly holds its hands close to its chest
at night.
Isn't this a children's toy?
We've been children since forever.
Dangerously.

One day my hands feel like an orphaned object.
I pick up a hand on the street
and when I take it out of my pocket in the evening, I'm starving.
I think my black pupils slowly turn white.

When I gather my hands in the evening
everyone's hands look the same.

ABOUT THE AUTHOR

Kim Haengsook is one of South Korea's eminent contemporary poets. She made her literary debut in 1999 and has published 5 poetry collections since, including most notably *What Errands Are You Running?* (2020), which won the prestigious Daesan Literary Award. Some of her poems have appeared in English in Poems of Kim Yideum, Kim Haengsook & Kim Min Jeong (Vagabond Press).

ABOUT THE TRANSLATORS

Susan K studied English literature and linguistics at the University of Toronto. After spending some years teaching English and managing people who teach English, she decided to walk the cold and lonely path of a freelance translator. She completed the Literature Translation Fellowship Program and the Media Translation Fellowship Program at the Literature Translation Institute of Korea and currently works as a full-time translator of poetry, webcomics, movies, and pretty much anything that interests her. She has also received a grant from the LTI to translate Park Soran's poetry collection, *One Person's Closed Door*. She loves all animals, but especially dogs; she loves all books, but especially mystery thrillers.

Léo-Thomas Brylowski graduated with a BA from the University of British Columbia and went on to complete the two-year LTI Korea Translation Academy fellowship program in Seoul. He was the Grand Prize recipient of the Korea Times Modern Korean Literature Translation Award in 2019 for his translation of Lee Kiho's short story "Choe Mijin, Where Have You Gone?" and has also received a grant from LTI Korea in 2020 for the translation of a novel by author Park Young (currently in progress; title is yet to be decided upon).

Hannah Quinn Hertzog graduated from the University of Washington with degrees in Korean, Asian Languages and Literature, and Computer Science, then went on to complete both the two-year fellowship program and the summer-long Media Translation fellowship program at the Literature Translation Institute of Korea. In 2020, she received the Grand Prize at the 51st Korea Times Modern Korean Literature Translation Awards for her translation of Kim Un-su's short story "Jab," as well as the LTI Korea Translation Award for Aspiring Translators for her translation of Hwang Jung-eun's short story "Gravedig." She currently works full-time as a software engineer in Seoul.

Joanne Park studied history at Yonsei University and finished the regular course program at LTI Korea. She lives with her cat in Seoul.

Soohyun Yang is a freelance translator and interpreter. Her translations have appeared in *Modern Poetry in Translation* (2016); *Korean Literature Now* (Winter 2019); and *The Poems of Hwang Yuwon, Ha Jaeyoun, and Seo Daekyung* (Vagabond Press, 2020); Seoul Wowbook Festival (2017); and Gothenburg Book Fair (2019).

Soeun Seo (she/they) is a poet and translator from South Korea and a Michener fellow. Their poems and translations have appeared in *Hayden's Ferry Review, Korean Literature Now, Guernica, Black Warrior Review*, etc. They co-translated *Hysteria* by Kim Yideum, which won the Lucien Stryk Award and the National Translation Award. Their latest translation, *Beautiful and Useless* by Kim Min Jeong, co-translated with Jake Levine, was published with Black Ocean.

Jiyoon Lee lives in Texas, likes hippy stuff, sings in a band, and likes dancing in the morning. Currently, she is busy learning how to become a small, fluffy white dog.

ACKNOWLEDGMENTS

_인간의 시간 : Human Time (Soohyun Yang)
_1984년이라는 미래 : The Future 1984 (Soohyun Yang)
_지하철 여행자 2084 : Underground Traveler 2084 (Soohyun Yang)
_천사에게 : Dear Angel (Soeun Seo)
_변신 : Metamorphosis (Soeun Seo)
_조각공원 : The Sculpture Garden (Jiyoon Lee)
_이별의 능력 : The Goodbye Ability (Jiyoon Lee)
_호르몬그래피 : Hormonography (Jiyoon Lee)
_성스러운 피 : Santa Sangre (Jiyoon Lee)
_목의 위치 : The Position of the Neck (Jiyoon Lee)

_ 1914년 4월 16일 : April 16, 1914 (Léo-Thomas Brylowski)
_그러나 : However (Léo-Thomas Brylowski)
_작은 집 : Little House (Léo-Thomas Brylowski)
_존재의 집 : House of Being (Léo-Thomas Brylowski)
_1월 1일 : January 1st (Léo-Thomas Brylowski)
_다정함의 세계 World of Kindness (Léo-Thomas Brylowski)
_유리창에의 매혹 Fascination for Windows (Léo-Thomas Brylowski)
_숲속의 키스 Kiss in the Forest (Léo-Thomas Brylowski)
_포옹: Embrace (Léo-Thomas Brylowski)
_침대가 말한다: The Bed Says (Léo-Thomas Brylowski)
_주택가: Residential Street (Léo-Thomas Brylowski)
_사라진 계단: Disappearing Staircase (Léo-Thomas Brylowski)
_초콜릿 분쇄기: Chocolate Grinder (Léo-Thomas Brylowski)

ABOUT THE SERIES

The Moon Country Korean Poetry Series publishes new English translations of contemporary Korean poetry by both mid-career and up-and-coming poets who debuted after the IMF crisis. By introducing work which comes out of our shared milieu, this series not only aims to widen the field of contemporary Korean poetry available in English translation, but also to challenge orientalist, neo-colonial, and national literature discourses. Our hope is that readers will inhabit these books as bodies of experience rather than view them as objects of knowledge, that they will allow themselves to be altered by them, and emerge from the page with eyes that seem to see "a world that belongs to another star."

*From the poem "Moon Country Mischief" by Kim Soo-young

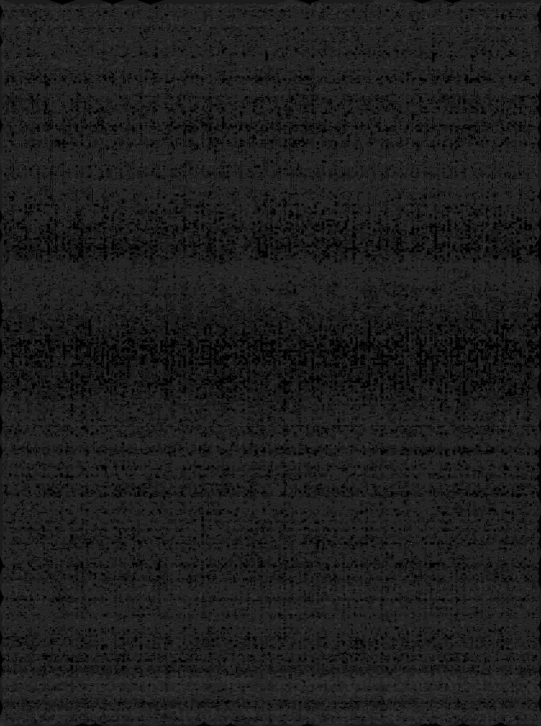